I'm Bigger Than You

BALBOA
PRESS

A DIVISION OF HAY HOUSE

Balboa Press books may be ordered through booksellers or by contacting:

Balboa Press
A Division of Hay House
1663 Liberty Drive
Bloomington, IN 47403
www.balboapress.com
1 (877) 407-4847

Because of the dynamic nature of the Internet, any web addresses or links contained in this book may have changed since publication and may no longer be valid. The views expressed in this work are solely those of the author and do not necessarily reflect the views of the publisher, and the publisher hereby disclaims any responsibility for them.

The author of this book does not dispense medical advice or prescribe the use of any technique as a form of treatment for physical, emotional, or medical problems without the advice of a physician, either directly or indirectly. The intent of the author is only to offer information of a general nature to help you in your quest for emotional and spiritual well-being. In the event you use any of the information in this book for yourself, which is your constitutional right, the author and the publisher assume no responsibility for your actions.

Any people depicted in stock imagery provided by Thinkstock are models, and such images are being used for illustrative purposes only.
Certain stock imagery © Thinkstock.

ISBN: 978-1-5043-8569-5 (sc)
ISBN: 978-1-5043-8570-1 (e)

Print information available on the last page.

Balboa Press rev. date: 08/16/2017

When I was little

I had a lot of

hard times

I lived in a home
that seemed so
cold and empty
and many times
even scary
I felt very alone

When I was in school
it seemed so busy
and I felt like I was
the only aware of
everyone being
distracted by
something else

Some people weren't very nice

Seems some people must have never noticed me

And some people went out of their way to notice people or get noticed

The halls could really seem longer some days

When I grew up
I worked
I worked a lot

One day I went back to the
the town I lived in when I
was small

I drove down the street I
used to live on

I drove passed the house
that used to be my home

I noticed how small
everything seemed
compared to my memories
as a child

I drove through the town that I used to feel overwhelmed in and realized that it never changed I grew

Things that seemed unreachable and miles away were just around the block

I realized that everyone can be bigger than they are on the outside

My heart is the same
size but it feels bigger

My mind still fits but

my thoughts are

bigger

My spirit which no one

can even see

is Bigger than outer

space

All of those things that used to come to mind that made me feel shrunken inside

I can now see above them

I tower above it all

I tell them

I AM BIGGER THAN YOU

I am brave because I'm bigger than you

I am confident because I'm bigger than you

I am going to be kind because I am bigger than you

I am going to make a difference because I'm bigger than you

I am going to live joyfully because I'm bigger than you

I am adorable and
wonderful and
designed
amazingly well
So, I will love me
Because I'm
bigger than you

I will forgive you because I'm bigger than you

I will treat you like my family because You are the same as Me

Printed in the United States
By Bookmasters